COOL
MILITARY GEAR

by Samantha S. Bell

Core Library

Imprint of Abdo
www.abdopublish

www.abdopublishing.com

Published by Abdo Publishing, a division of ABDO, PO Box 398166, Minneapolis, Minnesota 55439. Copyright © 2015 by Abdo Consulting Group, Inc. International copyrights reserved in all countries. No part of this book may be reproduced in any form without written permission from the publisher. Core Library™ is a trademark and logo of Abdo Publishing.

Printed in the United States of America, North Mankato, Minnesota
092014
012015

Cover Photo: Staff Sgt. Evelyn Chavez, US Air Force/US Department of Defense
Interior Photos: Staff Sgt. Evelyn Chavez, US Air Force/US Department of Defense, 1; Spc. Theodore Schmidt, US Army/US Department of Defense, 4; Staff Sgt. Sj Duga/Defense Video & Imagery Distribution System, 7; D. Myles Cullen, US Army/US Department of Defense, 9; Shutterstock Images, 12, 22 (right); North Wind Picture Archives, 15; Paul Thompson/National Geographic Society/Corbis, 18; Cpl. Alex C. Guerra, US Marine Corps/US Department of Defense, 20, 45; Andrew Kasten/Thinkstock, 22 (left); John Gomez/Thinkstock, 22 (center); US Army photo by Spc. Steven Young/Defense Video & Imagery Distribution System, 23; US Army photo by Spc. Matthew Freire/US Department of Defense, 25; Carl Schulze/AP Images, 29; US Army, 31; Melvin G. Tarpley/US Department of Defense, 33; SGT Kristina Truluck/ Defense Video & Imagery Distribution System, 35; Master Sgt. Lance Cheung, US Air Force/ US Department of Defense, 36; US Army photo by Spc. Jason Nolte/US Department of Defense, 38; Sayyid Azim/AP Images, 42; AP Images, 43

Editor: Lauren Coss
Series Designer: Becky Daum

Library of Congress Control Number: 2014944240

Cataloging-in-Publication Data
Bell, Samantha S.
 Cool military gear / Samantha S. Bell.
  p. cm. -- (Ready for military action)
 ISBN 978-1-62403-650-7 (lib. bdg.)
 Includes bibliographical references and index.
 1. United States--Uniforms--Juvenile literature. 2. United States--Equipment--Juvenile literature. 3. United States--Equipment and supplies--Juvenile literature.   I. Title.
 358--dc23
                                                                                    2014944240

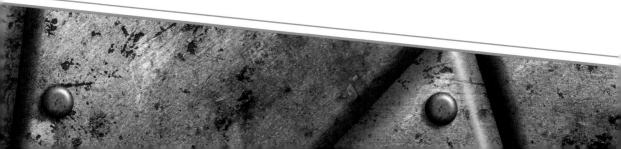

CONTENTS

CHAPTER ONE

REAL-LIFE HERO

The Korengal Valley in Afghanistan is a dangerous place for US soldiers. Enemy troops often hide in the area. But sometimes the missions take soldiers right through it. On October 23, 2007, the members of the 173rd Airborne Brigade were on night patrol in the valley. They were part of a mission to provide food, winter clothes, and medicine to people in Afghanistan who lived in remote villages.

The US military performs important missions in dangerous places around the world. Specialized gear helps them do their jobs and stay safe.

Staff Sergeant Salvatore "Sal" Giunta was part of the patrol. Like the other soldiers, he carried his gear in a rucksack on his back. Inside the rucksack were ammunition, grenades, night-vision goggles, a first-aid kit, water, climbing gear, and cold-weather gear.

Lifesaving Armor

Normally Giunta and the other soldiers would be wearing night-vision goggles on a mission like this. The goggles allow soldiers to see in almost total darkness. But the moon was full that night. The soldiers had enough light to see by. Suddenly,

Night-Vision Contacts

Night-vision technology is an important part of US military gear. Researchers are working on creating night-vision technology that is so small it can be built right into contact lenses! To work properly, night-vision equipment can't become overheated. The goggles have cooling units built in, making them larger and bulky. However, the new technology in the contacts doesn't need the cooling units. These infrared light sensors are made from a material that is as thin as a single carbon atom!

Body armor is designed to stop bullets. Sergeant Victor Roberts's vest saved his life when he was shot in the back in 2005.

gunfire broke out. They were being ambushed on three sides!

The two soldiers leading the platoon were hit. One of them was Giunta's best friend. A third was also wounded.

As Giunta was pulling that soldier to safety, a bullet shattered the weapon that he carried on his back. Another bullet hit Giunta right in the chest. But Giunta was wearing Interceptor Body Armor (IBA).

This armor consists of a vest that can protect against pistol rounds and fragments from grenades. The vest also has pockets with ceramic inserts, making the armor strong enough to stop high-velocity bullets. Giunta's armor worked, and he wasn't hurt. He kept going.

There were still two injured Americans up ahead, but enemy fire surrounded them. Giunta and his comrades began throwing grenades. The explosions provided cover as they ran to rescue the wounded. Finally, they reached the first soldier. He had been shot twice in the leg, and his gun was

First-Aid Kits

Since World War II, all soldiers have carried some type of first-aid kit in the field. For many years, all that was issued was a single compression bandage. Today, the kits include tourniquets, elastic bandages, adhesive tape, gauze, and gloves. They also contain special supplies that can be put directly on a wound. These may be a powder or a thin sponge. They help the blood clot faster. Then the wound seals up almost immediately. Other new additions to the kits include an eye shield, a special seal for chest wounds, and a strap cutter.

President Barack Obama, right, awarded Giunta, left, the Medal of Honor for his selfless actions. That is the highest honor any soldier can receive.

jammed. Other soldiers used their first-aid supplies to help him. But Giunta pushed on. His best friend was still down somewhere.

He was almost too late. When Giunta reached the top of a hill, he saw his wounded friend being dragged away by two enemy soldiers. Giunta charged forward and fired his gun, killing one of them. He shot again and wounded the other one. As that soldier ran off, Giunta reached his friend's side, removed his gear, and pulled him to cover. Giunta used the first-aid kit to keep his friend alive until help could arrive.

Many Kinds of Gear

Giunta's friend later died. Another soldier died as well. Without the body armor, Giunta probably would have been killed too.

The men and women in the US military must be ready for anything. They need special gear and tools to help them in combat. Some gear keeps them safe, just as the body armor protected Giunta when he was hit. US soldiers also have gear to use when attacking the enemy. Some gear is worn on their heads, some on their bodies, and some they carry with them. All of the gear helps US soldiers survive.

In 2011 Brigadier General Peter Fuller discussed the equipment soldiers were using on the battlefield:

> We have learned . . . that we fight not as individual Soldiers, but as members of a team, a squad—or Tactical Small Unit—with SSG Giunta's testimony [as] just one great example. This realization has provided a new way to look at how to outfit our Soldiers and opens up possibilities to lighten the weight of the individual by looking at its distribution among the members of these TSUs. Our doctrinal fighting load consists of 48 pounds; however it can range up to 120 pounds depending on the mission of the Soldier. The average load for our Soldiers operating in Afghanistan is 63 pounds, with many Soldiers carrying up to 130 pounds. The ability to distribute the individual Soldier's load across the TSU may be key to reducing their burden and ensuring overall physical and cognitive dominance.

Source: "Statement by Brigadier General Peter N. Fuller Before the Tactical Air and Land Forces Subcommittee." Armed Services Committee. Armed Services Committee, March 17, 2011. Accessed June 17, 2014.

Consider Your Audience

Consider how you would adapt this passage for a different audience, such as your parents, younger friends, or soldiers. Write a blog post conveying this same information for the new audience. How does your new approach differ from the original text and why?

GEAR THROUGH THE AGES

The military uses all kinds of complex equipment in battle. Some of the equipment is small enough for the troops to carry with them. This gear includes everything they might need on or off the battlefield.

Just as they do today, soldiers in the field thousands of years ago carried military gear. The first detailed records of military battles were found carved

A statue in Sparta, Greece, shows some of the gear used by ancient Greek warriors.

in stone by the ancient Sumerians in what is now Iraq. The 5,000-year-old carvings show that ancient Sumerian soldiers wore armored cloaks. They also wore copper helmets that were probably lined with leather.

As weapons and military tactics changed, the gear did too. Many battles in Greece were fought hand to hand, so their soldiers' gear consisted of a protective shield. Some also had helmets and armor if they could afford them. Heavier armor was eventually traded for lighter leather armor, allowing soldiers to move faster.

The First US Gear

The invention of the gun in the 1300s brought more changes. Armor was no longer an effective defense by the time the first American army, the Continental Army, was formed in 1775. Bullets could go right through it. These soldiers did not wear armor.

Most American soldiers during the Revolutionary War (1775–1783) were provided with small linen

A Continental soldier loads his musket with gunpowder from his powder horn.

haversacks. Carried over one shoulder, the haversack held food, eating utensils, a plate, and a cup. The larger knapsacks were worn on the back. They carried extra clothing and personal items. Ammunition was stored in a leather or tin cartridge box. Gunpowder was kept in a powder horn. Canteens for water were made of wood or tin. A blanket not only kept the soldier warm but also served as a tent if he didn't have one.

Civil War Haversacks

No matter what gear they left behind, Civil War soldiers could not go without their haversacks and canteens. Carried over one shoulder, a haversack held approximately three days of rations, or food. These included salt pork, salt, sugar, coffee, and hardtack, a type of bread. Canteens were made of tin and covered with blue or brown cloth to keep them cool. Every soldier also carried a tin cup, a metal plate, and eating utensils. Altogether, the gear weighed approximately 50 pounds (23 kg).

Inside a Civil War Knapsack

At the beginning of the Civil War (1861–1865), soldiers received supplies from their individual states. As the war went on, the equipment became more regular. Usually Union soldiers were better supplied than the Confederates. Much of the soldiers' equipment was worn on their belts. A cartridge box held ammunition. Scabbards held the bayonets.

Knapsacks were made of waterproof cloth or canvas. They held extra clothing and personal items. Each soldier also carried half a tent. He would team up with another soldier to make a full tent. A blanket or overcoat was strapped to the top of the knapsack.

US Gear Improves

In the years that followed the Civil War, US soldiers' gear was constantly redesigned to make it function better in the field. By World War I, haversacks had become part of a single pack, which was worn on a soldier's back. Shovels and aluminum canteens were strapped on the pack. But new types of weapons put the soldiers in greater danger. Shrapnel from explosives caused many serious injuries and deaths. Helmets were again used to protect the soldiers' heads. When the Germans began

Candy for Soldiers

US military rations advanced over the years. In 1937 soldiers in the Philippines were also among the first to test Hershey's new chocolate bars. This specially made candy didn't melt in the heat. However, it was to be eaten only in an emergency. In order not to tempt the soldiers, the candy didn't taste very good.

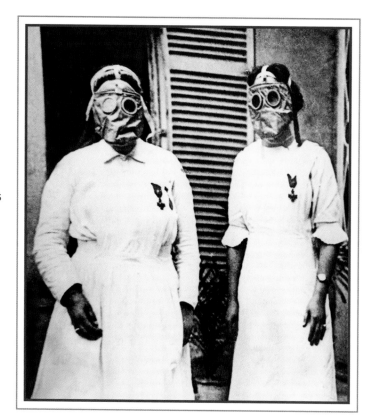

US nurses wear gas masks during World War I.

using poisonous gas as weapons, gas masks became standard issue as well.

During World War II (1939–1945), many US soldiers fought the Japanese on Pacific islands. Scientists worked to develop special supplies that could resist the water and mildew of the islands. One of the most useful items was a blanket-like rubber poncho. The poncho served as a raincoat, ground cover, and part of a shelter.

In 1943 an air force surgeon noticed that slow-moving missiles caused more than half of the wounds he treated. He began designing armor that protected against such missiles. By the time the United States entered the Korean War (1950–1953), a new type of vest had been developed. The nylon armor was used by all US troops on the front lines. More improvements followed. Today's soldiers have gear that not only uses the latest technology but also is practical for the battlefield.

FURTHER EVIDENCE

Chapter Two contains information about different types of military gear used throughout history. What was one of the chapter's main points? What evidence in the chapter supports this point? Check out the website at the link below. Find a quote from the website that supports the main idea of the chapter. Does the quote support an existing piece of evidence in the chapter? Does it add new evidence?

Battle of Agincourt
www.mycorelibrary.com/gear

CHAPTER THREE

HEAD GEAR

While the helmets of World War I shielded many of the troops from falling shell fragments, they didn't provide enough protection around the sides and the back. During World War II, the M1 steel helmet covered more of the head. The M1 was also used during the Korean War (1954–1975) and Vietnam War. In 1980 the Personal Armor System Ground Troops (PASGT)

Helmets, goggles, and other head gear play an important role in protecting US troops on the front lines.

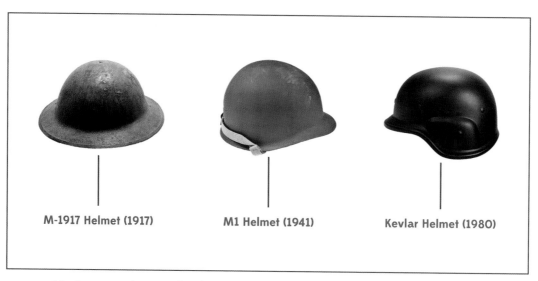

M-1917 Helmet (1917) M1 Helmet (1941) Kevlar Helmet (1980)

Helmets through the Ages

The helmets worn by US soldiers have gone through many changes. The graphic above shows some US military helmets and when they were introduced. How have helmets changed over time? How might have technology and other factors affected these changes?

helmet was introduced. Also known as the Kevlar or K-pot, this helmet was lighter and more comfortable than previous helmets. It was made of 19 layers of Kevlar, a fabric created to withstand heat and shrapnel. But even with all of these improvements, headgear for the soldiers continues to get better.

Helmets

Four types of helmets are currently being used by the military. All four are made of Kevlar. The Special

Green Berets, part of the US Special Operations Forces, wear MICH helmets on a training mission.

Operations Forces use the Modular Integrated Communications Helmet (MICH). It is lighter and stronger than the K-pot and can be adjusted to fit the wearer's head. It protects the head not only from shrapnel but from bullets as well. Other helmets include the US Marines' Lightweight Helmet (LWH) and the US Army's Advanced Combat Helmet (ACH). Providing even more protection for all the branches is the Enhanced Combat Helmet (ECH). All of these helmets are designed to work well with the new technology that is available.

Eye Protection

Threats and conditions on the modern battlefield have also led to changes in eye protection. In the 1980s, Navy SEALs began using goggles designed for downhill skiers. They kept smoke and debris from the eyes better than the military goggles did. Today, many private companies design goggles especially for soldiers. They've changed the shape of the goggles to fit the MICHs. The lenses are very strong. They protect soldiers from blast fragments, dust, sand, and wind. The goggles will even stop shotgun pellets from approximately 30 feet (9 m) away!

Night-Vision Goggles

Night-vision goggles allow soldiers to move and fight effectively in the

Sunglasses for Soldiers

Companies are also designing sunglasses for military use. Although wearing sunglasses was once considered a fashion statement, today they are a standard part of US military gear. They protect the eyes from ultraviolet radiation, infrared light, lasers, and side and front impacts.

Night-vision goggles allow US troops to perform missions at night or in darkness.

dark. Soldiers began using night-vision equipment in the late 1900s. The goggles are constantly being improved, making them stronger and lighter. The latest models allow soldiers to see infrared emissions. These rays cannot be seen with the human eye. Infrared emissions come from heat that radiates from people and warm engines. Some night-vision goggles consist of just a monocle. These fit over only one eye. Others are shaped more like binoculars. They can be mounted onto the MICHs or be handheld.

Protective Face Paint

Soldiers have used face paint to hide from the enemy for many years. But modern face paint may protect soldiers in other ways. When a bomb goes off, it sends a wave of heat that burns exposed skin. Scientists are creating a new type of paint to shield soldiers from this heat. Made of synthetic materials, the paint can protect skin up to 600 degrees Fahrenheit (316°C) for more than a minute. Even with just a thin layer, the soldier is much safer.

Gas Masks

Just like other weapons, chemical weapons have become more advanced over time. Gas masks are still issued to soldiers to protect them from these weapons. However, today the masks include lots of extras. Voice transmitters allow the soldiers to talk to one another. Drinking tubes can be connected directly to the soldier's canteen.

Some gas masks are designed with just one filter. The filter keeps toxic chemicals from entering the nose or mouth. Other masks have two smaller filters. These are created so they don't get in the way when soldiers fire a weapon.

North Atlantic Treaty Organization (NATO) advisors train pilots from Afghanistan how to use night-vision goggles (NVGs). The pilots are challenged by this new technology:

> "The 'goggles' phase . . . can be very challenging," said Chief Warrant Officer 4 Andy Miller, MD-530 team standardization pilot advisor. "Looking through NVGs is like looking with just one eye open and with everything in shades of just green and black. . . ."

> "The most important lesson that the students must learn is how to interpret what they see through the goggles," said Chief Warrant Officer 3 Lee Lane, MD-530 team standardization pilot advisor. "For example, they learn the science behind relative motion and to recognize that objects in the distance seem to stay the same while objects close up move quickly."

> Source: Capt. Anastasia Wasem. "Night Vision Training Increases Afghan AF Capabilities." US Air Force. Official United States Air Force Website, 2013. Web. Accessed June 4, 2014.

Back It Up

The author of this passage is making a point about night-vision goggles. Write a paragraph describing the point the author is making. Be sure to include two or three pieces of evidence the author uses to make the point.

CHAPTER FOUR

PROTECTING THE BODY AND STAYING DRY

Soldiers have found many different ways to protect their bodies throughout history. Armor worn by ancient Roman soldiers nearly 2,000 years ago was made of leather and steel. Today's soldiers wear armor too. Body armor has saved many lives. But it has its drawbacks. Even modern armor is heavy and hot. It limits a soldier's ability to move. If soldiers have to cover a lot of ground, the armor can

A US soldier wears Interceptor Body Armor while stationed in Iraq.

wear them down. However, as technology continues to improve, so does the armor.

Body Armor

The armor used by modern US soldiers is called Interceptor Body Armor (IBA). It's made of Kevlar and ceramic plates. IBA was first made in 1998. The foundation of the armor is a Kevlar tactical vest. By itself, the vest can protect the soldier from pistol shots and small grenade fragments. But for larger threats, such as rifle bullets, ceramic plates are added.

The plates are made of a lightweight but extremely strong material. Two plates for the front and back protect vital organs, including the heart, lungs, and liver, from direct impacts. The armor is made so that more plates can be added to protect the sides and other areas of the body. The vest also has straps that allow the soldier to add extra pouches for ammunition, grenades, and radios.

By itself, the vest weighs 8.5 pounds (4 kg). With the two main plates, it weighs 16.5 pounds (7 kg).

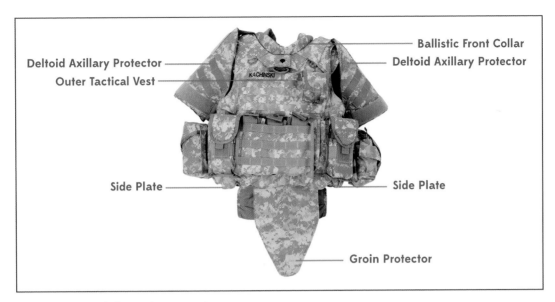

Ballistic Front Collar

Deltoid Axillary Protector

Deltoid Axillary Protector

Outer Tactical Vest

Side Plate

Side Plate

Groin Protector

Suited for the Environment

A soldier's body armor is designed to protect a soldier. Take a look at this diagram of a soldier's IBA. How might these different pieces protect a soldier in the field? How else could this IBA help a soldier?

The extra plates and gear can add 30 pounds (14 kg) or more to the armor. Besides making it heavier, these extra plates also make it hotter. Sometimes soldiers must choose between extra weight and extra protection.

CamelBak Canteen

While soldiers can leave some gear behind, they must take their canteens with them. The US military often works in hot, dry conditions. Without enough

Ghillie Suit

Scottish game officials called *ghillies* used to cover themselves with a tarp to hide from poachers, people who hunt animals illegally. Today's snipers, or shooters, wear ghillie suits when they need to blend in with the woods. These special uniforms have canvas sewn to the front and shredded burlap on the back. The burlap is often made to look like heavy foliage. Leaves and other vegetation can be attached to the suit. This allows the soldier to move undetected.

water, soldiers can't do their jobs well. Modern canteens are made of plastic. They are attached to a belt or rucksack. But many soldiers are also using a new kind of canteen, the CamelBak. The CamelBak system consists of a plastic water bag connected to a small hose. Both are placed in an insulated bag to keep the water from getting too hot. The bag is strapped onto a soldier's back or rucksack. The hose runs to the soldier's shoulder. Then the soldier can take a drink anytime without taking a break. Many soldiers carry both CamelBaks and

Ghillie suits help soldiers blend into trees, bushes, or other surroundings.

regular canteens. This way they will be sure to have enough water.

Gore-Tex Rain Gear

The military usually can't afford to postpone a mission because of bad weather. For decades soldiers used waterproof jackets and pants when it rained or snowed. But the material didn't allow air to pass through. The soldiers would become hot and sweaty. The waterproof material also made a lot of noise when the soldiers moved.

In the 1960s, a father-and-son team created a new type of fabric. They called it Gore-Tex. It was both breathable and waterproof. It had tiny holes that were large enough for air to pass through. But the holes were too small for water to go through. In 1977 a company began making tents and rain gear from Gore-Tex. In the 1980s, the military started issuing the new Gore-Tex rain gear to soldiers. Today, Gore-Tex jackets, pants, and boots are standard issue. This means they are given to every soldier.

Ponchos and Poncho Liners

Waterproof ponchos also keep soldiers dry in wet weather. But that's not all they do. Some soldiers use a poncho as a tarp to cover a pack when it rains.

Snivel Gear

"Pack light, freeze at night" is a common saying among soldiers. Sometimes a mission requires the soldiers take as little as possible. This means they have to leave all of their snivel gear behind. Snivel gear includes items that make a soldier more comfortable in the field, including rain gear, sleeping bags, ponchos, and liners.

A soldier relaxes with his poncho liner during a break. Some soldiers like the liners so much that they take them home when they leave the service.

A soldier can also make a shelter with the poncho by tying it to some trees.

Each poncho comes with a poncho liner. The poncho liner is very useful as well. The liner usually measures approximately 56 inches (142 cm) by 86 inches (218 cm). It is meant to be tied to the standard-issue poncho. The liner is lightweight and compact. It provides just the right amount of insulation for a cool night. When put together, the poncho and liner can be used as an emergency sleeping bag.

CHAPTER FIVE

TOOLS AND OTHER GEAR

Besides the protective gear they wear, US troops also carry special tools and equipment. Some of the gear helps them win in combat. Some of it helps them stay safe. Some of it helps them save others.

Entrenching Tool

Soldiers have used the entrenching tool, or e-tool, since World War I. The e-tool is actually a small shovel.

US soldiers in the field have to be ready for anything.

US soldiers in Afghanistan use their e-tools to prepare a construction site.

The top of the shovel folds down. This makes it compact enough to carry. The tool has a cover that attaches to the soldier's rucksack. The soldiers can use the e-tool to dig foxholes. They can also use it as a crowbar and even as a weapon if necessary. The e-tool is one of the heavier pieces of gear a soldier carries.

Flashlights

The US military doesn't stop working when the sun goes down. They must find ways to see and work in the darkness. Crookneck flashlights have been issued to soldiers for years. These flashlights are bent near the top to make them easy to carry and clip on a belt. Like other flashlights, the crookneck flashlight produces only white light. This is the type of light we see in the daytime. But new flashlights are being developed. The Streamlight Sidewinder flashlight is smaller and lighter. It produces not only white light but red light as well. Red light has the least effect on a person's night vision. Soldiers use

Multi-Tools

Campers, hikers, and others who enjoy the outdoors often carry pocketknives. Most soldiers will take along a multi-tool as well as a pocketknife. Multi-tools are similar to pocketknives, but they can do much more. They work as pliers, wire cutters, saws, screwdrivers, and files. Some kinds even include tools for preparing explosives. Because they are used so often, soldiers carry their multi-tools on their belts, where they can easily reach them.

The Nett Warrior System

Army Rangers and other soldiers are using the Nett Warrior system. This system helps leaders stay aware of what's happening on the battlefield. The centerpiece of the system is a chest-mounted smartphone. It displays the locations of fellow soldiers. The smartphone also allows text messages and other information to be passed between soldiers.

red light to read maps at night. When the light is turned off, they don't have to wait for their eyes to readjust to the darkness. This flashlight also has blue light for following blood trails. It even has infrared light for use with night-vision gear.

Personal Role Radios

Good communication is essential on the battlefield. Modern soldiers communicate using Personal Role Radios (PRRs). Just 3.5 inches (9 cm) by 5.5 inches (14 cm), these short-range radios can work up to a few hundred yards. They include a headset and a lightweight microphone. In conference mode, a commander can speak to all of the soldiers at once and hear their responses. In one-on-one mode, soldiers speak individually to one another. One PRR can also transfer data to another PRR.

The men and women of the US military have very tough jobs to do. The gear they use helps keep them as safe and comfortable as possible while in the field. As technology changes, the US military's gear continues improving. Scientists and engineers are constantly trying to come up with new gear to keep soldiers safe and effective on the front lines.

EXPLORE ONLINE

Private companies compete to develop the best multi-tools for soldiers. The website below compares several popular brands. As you know, every source is different. How is the information given in the website different from the information in the chapter? What information is the same? What can you learn from this website?

Multi-Tools Face Off
www.mycorelibrary.com/gear

A US Navy sailor patrols the Bainbridge.

Hostage Rescue

In 2009 four Somali pirates took US cargo ship captain Richard Phillips as a hostage off the coast of Somalia. Captain Phillips was held for several days in a lifeboat. US Navy officers on the ship the *Bainbridge* tried to negotiate with the pirates. At night, the navy sailors monitored the lifeboat with night-vision goggles. Eventually, Navy SEALs parachuted into the sea with inflatable boats.

The SEALs were prepared for anything. The captain was tied up, and one of the pirates pointed a gun at him. When it became clear the pirates were considering killing Phillips, the SEALs moved into action. They fixed their night-vision scopes on the lifeboat. They could see the captain. As soon as the pirates were in view, the SEALs shot and killed them. Phillips was saved.

Osama bin Laden

Finding Osama bin Laden

In May 2011, a team of Navy SEALs moved in on a compound in Abbottabad, Pakistan. Their mission was to capture or kill Osama bin Laden, who was in the compound. In 2001 bin Laden's terrorist organization had led an attack on the United States that claimed thousands of lives.

The SEALs were well prepared. They wore body armor, helmets, and gloves. They brought gear they might need, including multi-tools, CamelBaks, radios, maps, headsets, and first-aid kits. Two helicopters dropped the seals off near the compound. They went inside the dark house wearing night-vision goggles. The SEALs could make out the men, women, and children in the house. They could see who had weapons and who didn't. They searched the house room by room. On the third floor, they found bin Laden. The SEALs didn't hesitate. After years in hiding, bin Laden was shot and killed.

Why Do I Care?

Do you know anyone in the US military? Maybe you plan to join the military when you grow up. How does knowing about a soldier's gear affect you? Do you think it's an important subject to understand even if you aren't in the military? Why or why not?

Take a Stand

This book discusses how military gear helps keep US soldiers safe in the field. Imagine you have to convince the US government to spend money on only one kind of gear. Which type of gear do you think is the most important for the US government to invest in? Why? Use evidence from the book to support your argument.

Surprise Me

Chapters Three, Four, and Five identify different types of military gear used by soldiers today. Which types of gear did you find the most surprising? Write a few sentences about each one.

Tell the Tale

Chapter Two mentions the gear used by soldiers during the Civil War. Write 200 words telling the story of a Civil War soldier. Is he fighting for the North or the South? Describe his gear. How does he feel about the war? Be sure to set the scene, develop a sequence of events, and give a conclusion.

GLOSSARY

bayonet
a long knife attached to the muzzle end of a rifle

foliage
a mass of leaves from a plant

foxhole
a pit dug quickly to give a soldier cover from enemy fire

impact
to hit with force

infrared
rays of light that cannot be seen by the human eye without special equipment

monocle
an eyeglass for one eye

platoon
a military company consisting of two or more squads

rations
food allowances for one day

shrapnel
small pieces of debris that scatter from an explosion

sniper
a soldier who specializes at shooting long distances from a hidden place

Special Operations Forces
units of the US military that are specially trained for certain types of high-risk missions

tourniquet
a bandage that can be tied around an injured person above the wound to help stop bleeding

LEARN MORE

Books

Andrews, Simon. *Soldier*. New York: DK Publishing, 2009.

Hamilton, John. *The Army*. Edina, MN: ABDO, 2010.

Rasmussen, R. Kent. *World War I for Kids: A History with 21 Activities*. Chicago: Chicago Review Press, 2014.

Websites

To learn more about the US military and its resources, visit **booklinks.abdopublishing.com**. These links are routinely monitored and updated to provide the most current information available.

Visit **www.mycorelibrary.com** for free additional tools for teachers and students.

INDEX

ABOUT THE AUTHOR

Samantha Bell lives in the upstate of South Carolina with her family and lots of animals. She is the author and/or illustrator of more than 20 books for children. She is very thankful for the men and women of the US military.